Available now on Amazon!

CREAMY MCT, HOW TO MAKE IT

Would you like to save a lot of money creating one of the hottest supplements in the marketplace today using MCT oil?

Wacky Snacks and Sweet Sensations

An updated version of the original cookbook that sold thousands of copies. These recipes are **NOT** for those watching their weight!

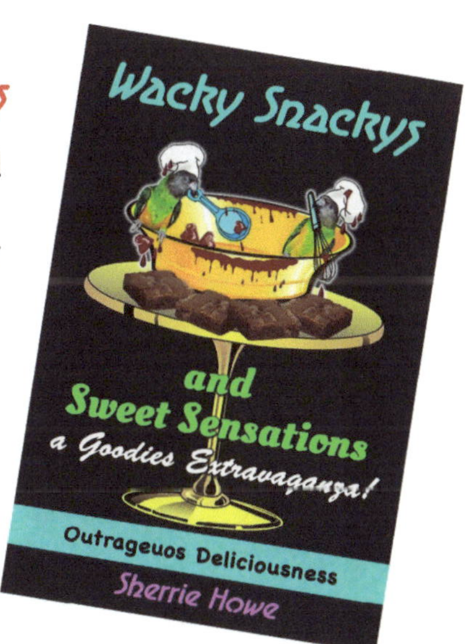

Coming soon:

Volume Two, No Nuts Here, using lowcarbfoods.me flour mix.

Low Carb Desserts
Low Carb Bread
Low Carb Snacks
NO NUTS IN HERE!
Volume 1
Includes 0 net carb sweets
LOW CARB FOODS
Low Carb Recipes Cookbook made with wheat flours for a Low Carb Ketogenic style eating plan. No nut flours used.
by Sherrie Howe

Table of Contents

Disclaimer:

The information in this book is not intended or implied to be a
substitute for professional medical advice, diagnosis or treatment.
All content, including text, graphics, images and information
contained in this book is for general information purposes only.
lowcarbfoods.me, and the author (Sherrie Howe) makes no
representation and assumes no responsibility for the accuracy of
Information contained in this book, and such information is subject
to change without notice. You are encouraged to confirm any
information obtained in this book with other sources, and review
all information regarding any medical condition or treatment with
your physician.

Results may vary due to measuring inconsistencies among people.
It is always best to weigh out your ingredients for consistent
results.

Sherrie

What is considered Lower Carbs?

What is considered low carb? Any digestible Carb (net carbs) count of 130 grams a day or below is considered low carb. If you are eating a regular Western diet, you can easily pack away 250 grams of carbs in a day, especially if some of those foods contain refined carbs including sugar.

Any eating program that reduces your carb intake is beneficial to help prevent diabetes, weight gain, insulin resistance, leptin resistance and many other life altering conditions.

Net carbs means digestible carbs. To figure this out, take the carb count of the food and subtract the fiber count, as fiber is not digested so they are not counted and you will have the net carb count. The grams of sugar alcohols are also subtracted. If you are on a strict low carb load like the keto diet (25 carbs or less), then you would only subtract half of the sugar alcohol carbs...if moderate to liberal (25 to 100), then you subtract all the sugar alcohol grams...as I did in this recipe guide. Net carbs listed on processed foods like chocolate bars can be misleading and have negative effects on your weight and blood sugar. Processed foods that have net carbs listed should be eaten with caution.

The Ketogenic weight loss program suggests 25 net carbs or under a day (strict) up to 50 grams a day (less restrictive) to put your body in a state of ketosis. The keto diet aims to force your body into using a different type of fuel instead of relying on sugar (glucose) that comes from carbohydrates (such as grains, legumes, vegetables, and fruits). The keto diet relies on ketone bodies, a type of fuel that the liver produces from stored fat. Eating low carb and high fat will enable your body to do this. The amount of weight and how fast you want to lose it depends on your macros, BMI and all kinds of factors. This information is readily available on the web. I Personally find this way of eating to be too restrictive, as it cuts out a lot of fruits which I find beneficial in the diet on several levels.

A Moderate low carb level is considered 25 to 50 net carbs per day.

A Liberal low carb intake would be considered 50 to 100 net carbs per day.

The recipes in this book focus strictly on net carb counts only. These recipes contain nutritional information for the **WHOLE** recipe, because portion sizes are different for all of us. Just divide the whole information by how many servings you desire. This flour mix is very simple and uses only 3 ingredients that taste and work similar to standard all purpose flour in recipes. Besides the recipes in this book, you can use it just like AP flour for some other applications such as thickening agents, breading foods to be fried or even a zero carb icing mix (recipe included) without the after taste of some of the powdered sugar alternatives.

Introduction to Lower Carb ingredients

Einkorn flour is the most ancient wheat, offering many essential dietary and trace minerals and this ancient grain also has less gluten (a different type) and more nutrition than traditional wheat. Americans now consume about 55 pounds of wheat flour every year. It isn't just the amount of wheat consumed that's of concern, but also the hidden components found within wheat that can cause weight gain and disease, due to constant hybridization and scientific engineering. Einkorn flour has many health benefits, including, reducing the risk of eye disease because it contains dietary carotenoids, helps with weight loss, reducing the risk of obesity due to better digestion, contains less gluten than standard wheat and limits allergy symptoms, just to name a few. Einkorn flour also contains less carbs (40% less) and more fiber than standard wheat flours.

Carbalose flour behaves similar to wheat flour but contains 80% less carbs. Carbalose is made mostly from wheat, yet it lacks most non-fiber carbohydrates. There are a lot of adjustments for liquids, leavening and baking times to use this flour. I have combined it with Einkorn to give you the best tasting similar products that we all know and love made from all-purpose flour. "Do NOT substitute Carb Quick" in these recipes. It will not work.

Einkorn Flour

Carbalose Flour

The sweeteners in these recipes are based on my particular likes. My go-to sweetener is a sugar alcohol called Xylitol. It is used one to one for sugar replacement. The "alcohol" in the name does not mean it contains alcohol. Sugar alcohols occur naturally in some foods such as fruits and berries and are also produced by altering the carbohydrates in these plants. Sugar alcohols do not contribute to tooth decay and are not absorbed by the body, which is why they are net carb free. Some types can leave you with some digestional discomfort if eating too much. Erythritol has been said to be the least likely to have this effect, but it is only about 70% as sweet as sugar and it leaves a cooling effect after taste in your mouth. Increasing the amount to make it as sweet as sugar also has drawbacks, as it will recrystallize in your finished products. You can use a combination of Erythritol and/or Xylitol and add Stevia. Whatever works for your personal taste is what you should use.

There have been no baked experiments in this book just using powdered stevia or like sweeteners. Some baked goods rely on sugar weight and non-hygroscopic sweeteners (does not absorb water from surrounding ingredients), which is why especially Xylitol and also Erythritol are ideal for baked goods.

If you choose to replace the sugar alcohol sweeteners with other sweeteners, your net carb count will change. Your preference of sweetener and how to use them is strictly up to you.
You will most likely need to order these ingredients online.

Xylitol, Erythritol, Einkorn Flour and Carbalose are all Non-GMO. products. You can purchase Non-GMO Vital Wheat Gluten.

Non-standard Ingredients you will need in this book include:
Carbalose Flour (Carbalose Flour comes in 3 lb. bags).
Einkorn All Purpose Flour (Einkorn All Purpose comes in 2 lb. bags).
Vital Wheat Gluten
Xylitol
Sukrin Gold (Erythritol brown sugar)

About the dough

When using this flour, the dough will be a little stickier than other dough's. This is due to the slow liquid absorption rate. Let the dough stand for a minute before kneading and only use a tiny amount of flour if needed to knead out. Only knead this dough 8-12 times.

Sticky dough   **Kneaded dough**

Ready to rise   **Risen dough**

Lowcarbfoods.me Low Carb Flour Mix Recipe

Weighing out ingredients for making this mix as well as when baking will yield better results!

5 Cups (475 grams) Carbalose Flour
3 1/4 Cups (400 grams) Einkorn Flour
5 Tablespoons (50 grams) Vital Wheat Gluten

1 cup lowcarbfoods.me flour mix weighs 108 grams
1 cup lowcarbfoods.me flour mix = 33.6 net carbs

Blend all ingredients until uniform. Store in airtight container.

Sandwich Bread

This bread has a crunchy crust. For a softer crust, you can use milk instead of water, but it will increase your net carb count by 15 for the loaf.

1 1/4 Cups + 1 Tablespoon warm water
1 Tablespoon Xylitol
5 teaspoons Instant Yeast
1 Egg, large, add liquid if needed to equal 1/4 cup
1 teaspoon Salt
3 3/4 Cups (Lowcarbfoods.me) Low Carb Flour mix

In small bowl, add yeast to water so it can proof. Set aside for 3-5 minutes.
Add salt and Xylitol to flour mix in a large bowl.
Put yeast mixture and egg in bowl and whisk until well mixed.
Add yeast mix to flour mix and stir. Dough will be sticky.
Turn onto floured surface and knead four to five times. Add only a tiny amount of flour mix if needed. When dough has smoothed out, put into a spray oiled bowl and cover with a warm towel and let rise in a warm place until doubled in size...about an hour.
Turn on oven to 375º.
When dough is done, punch down and form into a loaf and put into a 9x5 loaf pan to rise until doubled in size, about 30 minutes.

It is important to have your oven hot before putting the risen loaf in the oven. Bake for 35 - 40 minutes. Do NOT open door during first 20 minutes of baking time.

Nutritional information on page 9

Hamburger Buns

For Hamburger buns, use the Sandwich Bread recipe and after punching down the dough, cut into 6 - 8 pieces, depending on how big you want your rolls. Roll each piece into a ball and flatten. Lay on parchment paper lined pan to rise until double in size. Bake 15 - 20 minutes.

Pizza Crust

For Pizza Crust, use the Sandwich Bread recipe and after punching down the dough, cut into 3 pieces (thick crust) or 4 pieces (thin crust). Roll out to 10 - 12 inches. Lay on parchment paper lined pan to rise until double in size. Poke several places with fork for air to escape. Bake 12 - 15 minutes. Let cool for later or immediately add your favorite toppings and bake until done.

French Bread Style

For French bread use the Sandwich Bread recipe and after punching down the dough, cut into 3 - 4 pieces. Roll into logs about 7 inches long and cut 3 - 4 diagonal 1/4 inch deep slices on top. Lay on parchment paper lined pan to rise until double in size. Bake 20 - 25 minutes.

I did not do a good job dividing my dough equally

Sandwich Bread, Buns, Pizza crust, French Bread
Nutritional results for complete recipe as written

Cal	Carbs	Fiber	Fat	Protein	Sugar Alc	Net Carbs
1331.1	206.53	76.72	24.18	110.5	15	114.81

Cinnamon Rolls

Dough

1/2 Cup Milk, warm
1/4 Cup Water, warm
2 Tablespoons Xylitol
4 teaspoons instant yeast
1 Egg, large, add liquid to equal 1/4 cup
1/2 teaspoon Salt
2 1/4 Cups (Lowcarbfoods.me) Low Carb Flour mix

Filling

2/3 cup Sukrin Gold (Erythritol Brown Sugar) not packed
1 Tablespoon Cinnamon
1/4 Cup Butter, melted
1/4 Cup Heavy Cream, room temperature (optional)

Directions:

In small bowl, add yeast to water so it can proof. Set aside for 3-5 minutes.

Add salt and sweetener to flour mix.

Put yeast mixture, milk and egg in bowl and whisk until well mixed. Add flour mix and stir. Dough will be sticky. Turn onto floured surface and knead four to five times. Add only a tiny amount of flour mix if needed. When dough has smoothed out, put into a spray oiled bowl and cover with a warm wet towel and let rise in a warm place until doubled in size...about an hour. (I like to put the dough in a plastic rectangular container so it is already the correct shape to flatten out for the rolls).

Mix Sukrin Gold and brown sugar and set aside.

Preheat oven to 375º.

When dough is done, punch down and flatten or roll out to a 9 x 12 rectangle. Spread on 1/2 of the melted butter. Sprinkle on the cinnamon sugar mix and then top with the rest of the melted butter.

Starting from the long side, roll the dough up to a cylinder. Roll as tight as you can. Put the seam side down.

Cut in halves until you have 8 pieces. Lay rolls in a 10 x 10 spray oiled pan.

Let rise about 30 minutes until double in size. Gently pour heavy cream over rolls if desired. This makes your rolls even softer. Let cream soak into rolls for about 5 minutes. It is important to have your oven hot before putting the risen rolls in the oven.
Bake for 25 - 30 minutes.

Do NOT open door during first 15 minutes of baking time.

Cinnamon Rolls

Nutritional results for complete recipe as written

Cal	Carb	Fiber	Fat	Protein	Sugar Alc	Net Carbs
1577.06	138.37	48.06	90.79	74.88	72.4	17.91

Most Moist Biscuits

1 1/4 Cups (Lowcarbfoods.me) Low Carb Flour mix
1/2 teaspoon Baking Soda
1/2 teaspoon Baking Powder
3 Tablespoons Butter, cold
1/2 Cup Greek Yogurt, full fat
1/2 Cup Heavy Cream
1/4 teaspoon salt

Turn on oven to 400º.

Mix the flour, salt, baking soda and baking powder together.
With a pastry blender, cut in butter until it resembles coarse meal.
I find using a shredder for the butter is easier.

Mix Yogurt and Heavy Cream together and then add to flour mix.
Mix lightly until almost moistened.

Turn onto floured surface and knead 7 - 8 times. Flatten the
dough to 1/2 inch thick. Cut with biscuit cutter or knife. Ball up
and flatten the scraps. Handle dough as little as possible so
biscuits don't get tough.

Bake on cookie sheet for 12 - 15 minutes

Most Moist Biscuits
Nutritional results for complete recipe as written

Cal	Carb	Fiber	Fat	Protein	Sugar Alc	Net Carbs
1201.7	70.28	24.18	94.16	42.56	0	46.1

Easy Flaky Pie Crust
(single large pie crust for 9" pie)

1 1/4 cups (Lowcarbfoods.me) Low Carb Flour mix
1/2 teaspoon Salt
1 teaspoon Xylitol
1 stick Butter, Chilled, Unsalted
1 Tablespoon + 1 teaspoon Ice Water
If using salted butter, omit salt.

Mix the flour, salt and sugar together. With a pastry blender, cut in butter until it resembles coarse meal.
I find using a shredder for the butter is easier.

Add ice water and work with hands until dough comes together. Flatten the dough into a disc, wrap in plastic wrap and refrigerate at least an hour.

To form pie shell, roll the dough on a floured surface to 12 - 14 inches.

Carefully put into pie pan and use as desired. This recipe makes wonderful turnovers as well.

Someone ate the pretty one before I could take a picture!

Easy Flaky Pie Crust
Nutritional results for complete recipe as written

Cal	Carb	Fiber	Fat	Protein	Sugar Alc	Net Carbs
1212.3	66.25	24.18	98.26	33.16	5	37.07

Polish Drop Noodles

1 1/2 Cups (Lowcarbfoods.me) Low Carb Flour mix
1 Egg, large
3/4 Cup Water
1/4 teaspoon Salt

Bring to a boil, 3 - 4 quarts of water with a Tablespoon of salt and a splash of oil. Make noodle batter while waiting for water to boil.

In bowl, combine flour mix, salt and egg. Slowly add the 3/4 cup of water and beat by hand until blended.

With a metal spoon form little dumplings about the size of an almond and drop into the boiling water. Turn water to low simmer and boil for 2-3 minutes after they float to the top.
Remove noodles with strainer.

Makes 2 1/2 cups dumpling noodles.

Polish Drop Noodles
Nutritional results for complete recipe as written

Cal	Carb	Fiber	Fat	Protein	Sugar Alc	Net Carbs
541.64	79.79	29.02	12.29	44.93	0	50.77

Basic Quick Bread

You may leave out the xylitol and make savory herb type breads too, but this will change your net carb count. Without sweetener, the net carb count for this recipe would be 23.

1 Cup (Lowcarbfoods.me) Low Carb Flour mix
1/4 Cup Xylitol
3/4 teaspoon Baking Powder
1/4 teaspoon Baking Soda
1/2 teaspoon Salt
1/4 Cup Greek Yogurt, full fat
1/2 Cup Milk or Cream
1 Egg, large
2 Tablespoons Butter, melted

Heat oven to 350º. Grease or spray oil 2 mini loaf pans.
Whisk together flour, Xylitol, baking powder, baking soda, and salt. Set aside.
Mix together the yogurt and milk or cream. Add egg and melted butter and whisk until mixed.

Add the wet ingredients to the dry ingredients and mix only until the flour has been incorporated into the batter. Do NOT over mix. Pour into the prepared pans and bake 25-30 minutes. Feel free to add your own berries, nuts or other additions, making sure to add the included net carbs.

Basic Quick Bread
Nutritional results for complete recipe as written

Cal	Carb	Fiber	Fat	Protein	Sugar Alc	Net Carbs
837.26	61.96	19.35	38.96	41.22	60	0

Banana Bread

1 Cup (Lowcarbfoods.me) Low Carb Flour mix
3/4 Cup Banana, mashed
1 Egg, large
4 Tablespoons Butter, softened
1 Tablespoon Milk
1/2 teaspoon Cinnamon
1/2 teaspoon Baking Powder
1/2 teaspoon Baking Soda
1/2 teaspoon Salt
1/2 Cup Xylitol

Turn oven on to 325º.

Mix the flour mix, cinnamon, baking powder, baking soda and salt. Set aside.

In bowl, beat butter and Xylitol until fluffy. Add egg and whip 20 seconds. Fold in mashed banana and milk.

Add the dry mix and stir just until moistened. Spray oil two mini loaf pans. Divide batter between the two pans.
This bread is super moist.

Bake for 35 - 40 minutes.

Banana Bread
Nutritional results for complete recipe as written

Cal	Carb	Fiber	Fat	Protein	Sugar Alc	Net Carbs
1204.88	94.08	24.3	57.01	35.3	120	0

Brownie Cake

1 Cup Xylitol
1 Cup (Lowcarbfoods.me) Low Carb Flour mix
6 Tablespoons Cocoa Powder
3/4 teaspoon Baking Powder
1 teaspoon Baking Soda
1/4 teaspoon Salt
1 Egg, large
1/2 Cup Milk
1/4 Cup Olive Oil
1 teaspoon Vanilla Extract
1/2 Cup Boiling Water

Preheat oven to 350°.

Grease and flour or spray oil an 8x8 or 9x9pan.

In a large bowl, combine sugar, flour, cocoa, baking powder, baking soda and salt.

Add egg, milk, oil and vanilla to dry mixture and mix with an electric mixer on medium for about 2 minutes.

Gently mix in boiling water. Batter will be very thin.

Pour into pan and bake 25 - 30 minutes. Cool on wire racks.

Brownie Cake
Nutritional results for complete recipe as written

Cal	Carb	Fiber	Fat	Protein	Sugar Alc	Net Carbs
1500.76	78.3	30.15	72.25	42.34	240	0

Super Moist Chocolate Cake

2 Cups (Lowcarbfoods.me) Low Carb Flour mix
1/2 Cup Xylitol
3 Packets Stevia Sweetener
6 Tablespoons Cocoa Powder
2 teaspoons Baking Soda
1 Cup Water
1 Egg, large
1 Cup Mayonnaise
1 teaspoon Vanilla Extract

Preheat oven to 350º.

Spray oil a 9x9 inch baking pan.

Whisk dry ingredients together in medium mixing bowl.

Add the water, mayonnaise, egg, vanilla and mix until evenly combined.

Pour batter into prepared baking pan.

Bake for 35 - 40 minutes or until toothpick comes out clean.

Super Moist Chocolate Cake
Nutritional results for complete recipe as written

Cal	Carb	Fiber	Fat	Protein	Sugar Alc	Net Carbs
2621.52	124.37	49.5	195.2	64.17	120	0

Awesome Icing
(This icing is not overly sweet and is light and fluffy.)

5 Tablespoons (Lowcarbfoods.me) Low Carb Flour mix
1 Cup Milk
1/2 Cup Butter, softened
1/2 Cup Shortening
1 Cup Xylitol
1/2 teaspoon Salt
1/2 teaspoon Vanilla

In saucepan, combine the flour and milk and cook until thick. Cover and set aside to cool.

In mixing bowl, combine sugar, Crisco, salt, butter, and vanilla and beat until fluffy.

Add cooked flour mixture and beat until creamy (you will want to use a stand mixer as this will take several minutes as Xylitol takes longer to dissolve than sugar).

You can use all butter instead of half shortening if you prefer, but icing will not be as stiff and have a lower melting point.

Awesome Icing
Nutritional results for complete recipe as written

Cal	Carb	Fiber	Fat	Protein	Sugar Alc	Net Carbs
2431.42	28.18	6.04	149.6	16.87	240	0

Soft Sour Cream Cookies

2 Cups (Lowcarbfoods.me) Low Carb Flour mix
1 teaspoon Baking Powder
1/2 teaspoon Baking Soda
1/2 teaspoon Salt
1/2 Cup Butter, softened
1/2 Cup Xylitol
2 Packets Stevia Sweetener
1 Egg, large
3/4 Cup Sour Cream
1 teaspoon Vanilla Extract
2 Cups Rhubarb, chopped, - optional

Preheat the oven to 350º

Line two baking sheets with parchment paper.

In a medium bowl, whisk together the flour, baking powder, baking soda, and salt.

In a large bowl, beat the butter, xylitol and stevia together with an electric mixer at medium speed until light and fluffy.

Add the egg and beat to combine.

Beat in the sour cream and vanilla, making sure all the ingredients are well combined.

Add 1/3 of the flour mixture at a time until all is combined.

Stir in the rhubarb, optional.

Drop tablespoons of batter onto the prepared baking sheets, spacing them about 2 inches apart.

Bake 10 to 12 minutes, until the edges of the cookies start to brown and the tops of the cookies get a little color. Let cool slightly, then remove to a cooling rack.

If using Air-bake pans, plain cookies will take 14-16 minutes, and with rhubarb, 16-18 minutes.

Soft Sour Cream Cookies
Nutritional results for complete recipe as written

Cal	Carb	Fiber	Fat	Protein	Sugar Alc	Net Carbs
2165.52	121	40.9	143.4	115.1	120	0

Deep Dish Berry Cobbler

Batter

1/2 Cup Xylitol
2 Packets Stevia Sweetener
1/2 Cup Butter, melted
1 1/2 Cups (Lowcarbfoods.me) Low Carb Flour mix
1 1/2 teaspoons Baking Powder
1/4 teaspoon Baking Soda
1/4 teaspoon Salt
1 teaspoon Vanilla Extract
1 Cup Milk

Berry Topping

1/2 Cup Xylitol
2/3 Cup Blueberries, frozen
2/3 Cup Blackberries, frozen
2/3 Cup Raspberries, frozen

Preheat oven to 350º

Spray oil a 2-quart baking dish and pour in melted butter.

For the Batter, in a large mixing bowl, combine flour mix, Xylitol,
Stevia, baking powder, baking soda and salt.
Stir in Milk and mix until well combined.
Pour mixture into baking dish. DO NOT STIR.

In another bowl, combine the Berries and Xylitol, mix lightly and
spoon over batter. DO NOT STIR!

Bake 45-60 minutes until crust rises to the top and browns.

Deep Dish Berry Cobbler
Nutritional results for complete recipe as written

Cal	Carb	Fiber	Fat	Protein	Sugar Alc	Net Carbs
2063.92	125.96	41.74	108.7	50.48	240	0

Old Fashioned Pancakes
(Small Batch, 8 pancakes)

3/4 Cup (Lowcarbfoods.me) Low Carb Flour mix
1 3/4 teaspoons Baking Powder
1/2 teaspoon Salt
1 Tablespoon Xylitol
1/2 Cup + 2 Tablespoons Milk
1 Egg, large
2 Tablespoons Butter, melted

In a large bowl, stir together the flour mix, baking powder, salt and sugar.

Make a well in the center and pour in the milk, egg and melted butter; mix until smooth.

Heat a lightly oiled griddle or frying pan over medium high heat.

Pour or scoop the batter onto the griddle, using approximately 1/4 cup for each pancake.

Brown on both sides and serve hot.

Old Fashioned Pancakes
Nutritional results for complete recipe as written

Cal	Carb	Fiber	Fat	Protein	Sugar Alc	Net Carbs
636.55	49.21	14.51	35.98	15.1	15	19.17

In Conclusion:

While I try hard to maintain complete accuracy, I am only as good as the information provided to me in databases and on labels. I find many inaccuracies on food labels and there is no one to over see that these companies are adhering to labeling laws. Our foods have been laced with additives to keep us addicted to their foods, sugar being one of the most heinous.

I hope these recipes fit the bill for a little healthier eating for the breads and sweets we crave.

This flour mix also makes a great breading. For an extra crispy breading mix, add 2 Tablespoons of Whey Protein Isolate to 1 cup lowcarbfoods.me flour mix. You can purchase a carb free variety.

Experiment with your own favorites. There are pages at the end of the book for your super creations.

Coming soon, lowcarbfoods.me website. Submit your favorite recipes to lowcarbfoods.me@gmail.com and we will test your recipe and give you credit.

Look for volume two, coming soon.

If you have any questions or concerns, please visit us on the web, lowcarbfoods.me (coming soon) and collect the free recipes.

Healthy eating to you

Sherrie Howe

My Awesome Creations

Recipe Name: Date:

My Awesome Creations

Recipe Name: Date:

My Awesome Creations

Recipe Name: Date: